Requests for information should be addressed to:

Zondervan Publishing House
Mail Drop B20
Grand Rapids, Michigan 49530
http://www.zondervan.com

Senior Editor: Caroline Blauwkamp
Creative Director: Patricia Matthews
Project Editor: Pat Matuszak
Design: Chris Gannon

Printed in China
98 99 00 /HK/ 3 2 1

FOR:

Kathy

With heartfelt love,

FROM:

Debbie

2-26-01

Each bright day has its sunset

And each rainbow has its end,

But no cloud can hide the light

Of my dear and trusted friend.

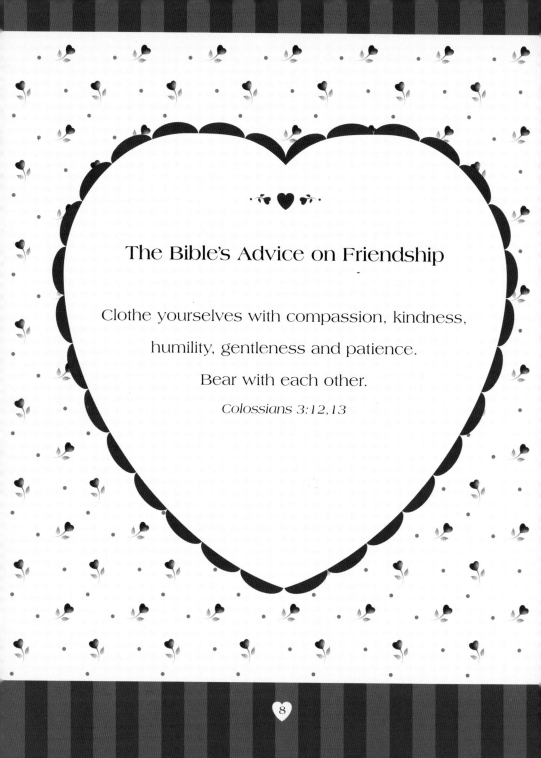

The Bible's Advice on Friendship

Clothe yourselves with compassion, kindness,

humility, gentleness and patience.

Bear with each other.

Colossians 3:12,13

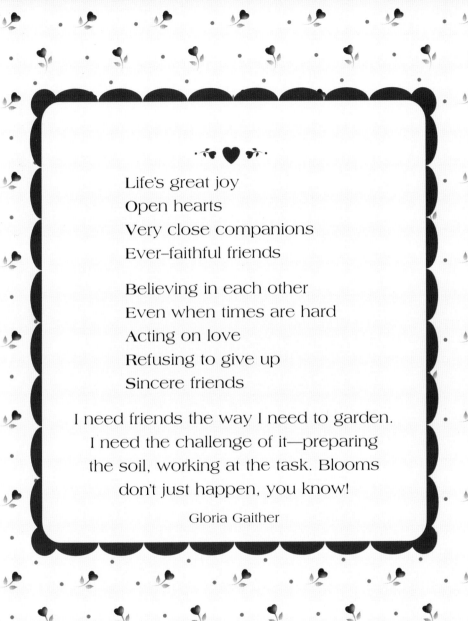

Life's great joy
Open hearts
Very close companions
Ever–faithful friends

Believing in each other
Even when times are hard
Acting on love
Refusing to give up
Sincere friends

I need friends the way I need to garden.
I need the challenge of it—preparing
the soil, working at the task. Blooms
don't just happen, you know!

Gloria Gaither

We're born into certain families,
with our relatives and our looks
already decided for us, but our
friends come to us because of our
own choice—and theirs!

The Soul selects her own Society.

Emily Dickinson

A friend is a present which
you give yourself.

Robert Louis Stevenson

A friend stands by
When storm clouds fly.
She's there through thick and thin.
And when you really need some help
She even steps right in.

A friend loves at all times.

Proverbs 17:17

God has said, "Never will I leave you; never will I forsake you." So we say with confidence, "The Lord is my helper; I will not be afraid."

Hebrews 13:5,6

God is love.

1 John 4:8

Jesus is a friend with whom you can feel safe.

Joni Eareckson Tada

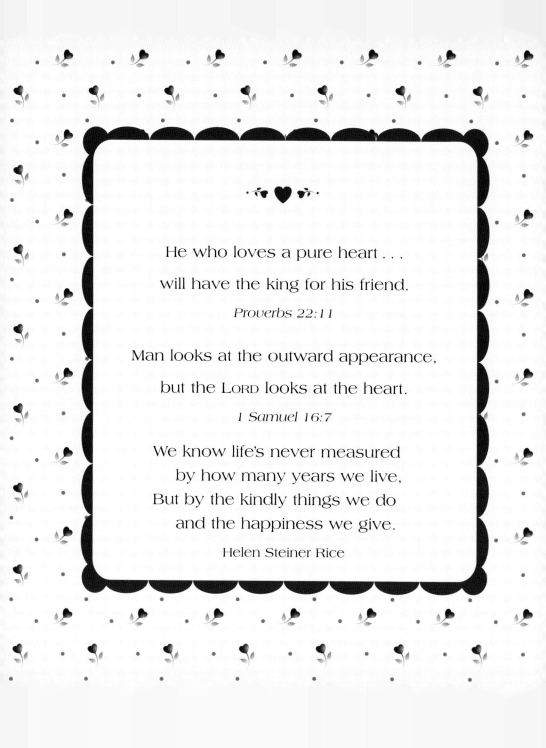

He who loves a pure heart . . .

will have the king for his friend.

Proverbs 22:11

Man looks at the outward appearance,

but the Lord looks at the heart.

1 Samuel 16:7

We know life's never measured
by how many years we live,
But by the kindly things we do
and the happiness we give.

Helen Steiner Rice

I like to think of the hand of my grandmother.
She would bring her hand down in the darkness
as she stood over my bed before I slept. I was ten.
She was eighty. She'd place her hand on
my head and offer a blessing in Flemish:
"A cross and a sleep well," she'd whisper.

Christopher de Vinck

No one has ever seen God; but if we
love one another, God lives in us and
his love is made complete in us.

1 John 4:12

The happiness of life is made
up of minute fractions—
a kiss or smile, a kind look,
a heartfelt compliment.

William Scott

A cheerful heart is good medicine.

Proverbs 17:22

Fun is a mystery that can't be trapped like an animal or caught like the flu. It comes without bidding if you have eyes to see it. Learn to find fun in unlikely places.

Barbara Johnson

Blessings abound—look around you. The smiles of children, the beauty of a glorious sunset, the comfort of a warm bed at night. Small and great, there are plenty of reasons to say to God, "Thank you."

Joni Eareckson Tada

Caring and sharing are

the very nicest parts of love.

Roy Lessin

This is how God showed

his love among us: He sent his

one and only Son into the world

that we might live through him.

1 John 4:9

We win by tenderness;

we conquer by forgiveness.

Frederick William Robertson

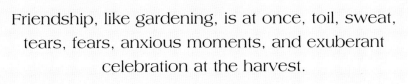

Friendship, like gardening, is at once, toil, sweat, tears, fears, anxious moments, and exuberant celebration at the harvest.

Gloria Gaither

Keep on loving each other. . . .
Do not forget to entertain strangers,
for by so doing some people have
entertained angels without
knowing it.

Hebrews 13:1–2

The commandments . . . are
summed up in this one rule:
"Love your neighbor as yourself."

Romans 13:9

The hands of God will hold us
close in ways that no earthly friend
ever could. You have a Father . . .
Lover . . . Friend . . . and Home in
heaven. God is as near as you'll
allow Him to be.

Mary Pielenz Hampton

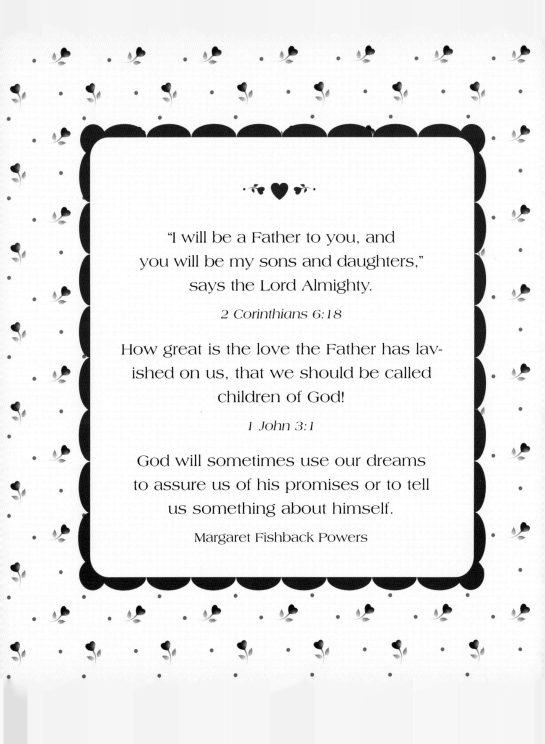

"I will be a Father to you, and
you will be my sons and daughters,"
says the Lord Almighty.

2 Corinthians 6:18

How great is the love the Father has lav-
ished on us, that we should be called
children of God!

1 John 3:1

God will sometimes use our dreams
to assure us of his promises or to tell
us something about himself.

Margaret Fishback Powers

You are you. God made you, you.
And you are exactly who He wants
you to be. Don't be somebody's clone.
The person you're trying to be may
very well be trying to be you!

Luci Swindoll

Your hands made me and

formed me. . . . May your unfailing

love be my comfort.

Psalm 119:73, 76

We love because he (God) first loved us.

1 John 4:19

It is in giving that we receive; it is in pardoning that we are pardoned.

Saint Francis of Assisi

Dear friends, since God so loved us, we also ought to love one another.

1 John 4:11

God is love. Whoever lives in love lives in God, and God in him.

1 John 4:16

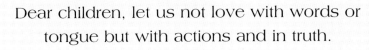

Dear children, let us not love with words or tongue but with actions and in truth.

1 John 3:18

Whoever loves God must also love his brother.

1 John 4:21

If I speak in the tongues of men and of angels, but have not love, I am only a resounding gong or a clanging cymbal.

1 Corinthians 13:1

Love never fails.

1 Corinthians 13:8

Follow the way of love.

1 Corinthians 14:1

Love does no harm
to its neighbor. Therefore love
is the fulfillment of the law.

Romans 13:10

Yes, call me by my pet name! let me hear
The name I used to run at, when a child,
From innocent play, and leave the cowslips
  piled,
To glance up in some face that proved me
  dear
With the look of its eyes. I miss the clear
Fond voices which, being drawn and recon-
  ciled
Into the music of Heaven's undefiled,
Call me no longer.
Yes, call me by that name, and I, in truth,
With the same heart, will answer and not wait.

Elizabeth Barrett Browning

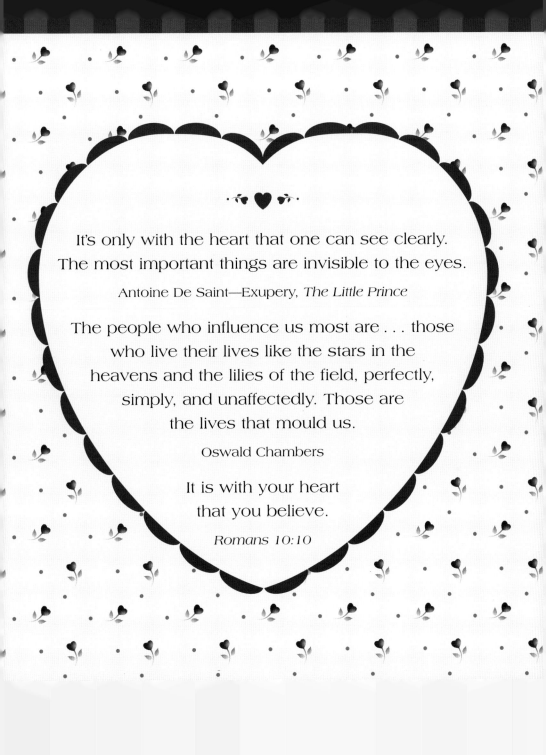

It's only with the heart that one can see clearly.
The most important things are invisible to the eyes.

Antoine De Saint—Exupery, *The Little Prince*

The people who influence us most are . . . those
who live their lives like the stars in the
heavens and the lilies of the field, perfectly,
simply, and unaffectedly. Those are
the lives that mould us.

Oswald Chambers

It is with your heart
that you believe.

Romans 10:10

Lord, make me an instrument
of Your peace. Where there is hatred
let me sow love; where there is injury,
pardon; where there is doubt, faith;
where there is despair, hope;
where there is darkness, light; and
where there is sadness, joy.

Saint Francis of Assisi

May the God who gives . . .
encouragement give you a spirit of
unity among yourselves as you follow
Christ Jesus, so that with one heart and
mouth you may glorify the God and
Father of our Lord Jesus Christ.

Romans 15:5,6

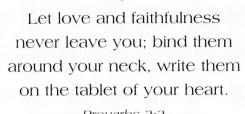

Let love and faithfulness
never leave you; bind them
around your neck, write them
on the tablet of your heart.

Proverbs 3:3

Children have a lot to offer us.
They don't have agendas, but
they do have hope and a simple
view of life. They are quick to
trust and slow to dislike others.

Barbara Johnson

God is greater than our hearts,
and he knows everything.

1 John 3:20

Lord, you have made us
for yourself, and our heart is
restless till it rests in you.

Saint Augustine

Christ's love compels us.

2 Corinthians 5:14

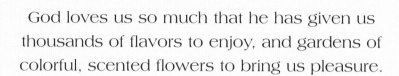

God loves us so much that he has given us thousands of flavors to enjoy, and gardens of colorful, scented flowers to bring us pleasure.

Terry Willits

A pleasant word is a bright ray of sunshine on a saddened heart. Therefore, give others the sunshine, and tell Jesus the rest.

L. B. Cowman

God has poured out his love into our hearts by the Holy Spirit.

Romans 5:5

The things we do today—
sowing seeds, or sharing simple
truths of Christ—people will
someday refer to as the first things that
prompted them to think of Him.

George Matheson

The word *trust* is the heart
of faith. It conveys an act of the will.
Trust sees and feels, and it leans on
those who have a great, living, and
genuine heart of love.

L. B. Cowman

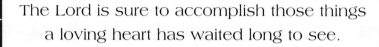

The Lord is sure to accomplish those things
a loving heart has waited long to see.

Bessie Porter

Every good and perfect gift
is from above, coming down from
the Father of the heavenly lights.

James 1:17

My entire heart does not have even
a hint of thirst. God has conquered everything within me through His love.

Lady Huntington

Because they are so passionately in love with God, the angels are perfectly conformed to His will. Whatever He tells them to do they do. Whoever He loves, they can't help but love. Because God cares for us so deeply, we can claim the wonderful friendship of angels.

Ann Spangler

The earth is full of his unfailing love. By the word of the LORD were the heavens made, their starry host by the breath of his mouth.

Psalm 33:6, 5

The LORD appeared to us in the past, saying: "I have loved you with an everlasting love; I have drawn you with loving—kindness."

Jeremiah 31:3

If we should cast the gift of a loving
thought into the heart of a friend,
that giving as the angels give.

George MacDonald

Sometimes a light surprises
The Christian while he sings;
It is the Lord who rises
With healing on His wings.
When comforts are declining,
He grants the soul again
A season of clear shining
To cheer it after rain.

William Cowper

O hearts of love! O souls that turn
Like sunflowers to the pure and best!
To you the truth is manifest;
For they the mind of Christ discern
Who lean like John upon His breast!

John Greenleaf Whittier

We can't gather up moments and store
them for later use. We can't anticipate the
time to come and catch it before it slips
away. Time can't be banked or hoarded—
the best we can do is make the most of
what time we do have.

Mary Pielenz Hampton

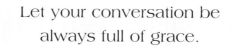

Let your conversation be
always full of grace.

Colossians 4:6

So let us love, dear Love, like as we ought.
Love is the lesson which the Lord us taught.

Edmund Spenser

It is the simple things of life that make
living worthwhile, the sweet fundamental
things such as love and duty, work and
rest, and living close to nature.

Laura Ingalls Wilder

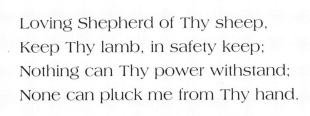

Loving Shepherd of Thy sheep,
Keep Thy lamb, in safety keep;
Nothing can Thy power withstand;
None can pluck me from Thy hand.

Jane Leeson

Appropriate use of touch can be more important than words. It can say things that words cannot easily say—such as "I'm here, today, in your present situation and I care about you."

Margaret Gill

All are needed by each one;
Nothing is fair or good alone.

Ralph Waldo Emerson

You . . . are a letter from Christ, . . .

written not with ink but with the Spirit of

the living God, not on tablets of stone

but on tablets of human hearts.

2 Corinthians 3:3

We who are willing to be used
also impart a legacy of Christ's love in
the lives of those we encounter. As the
old saying goes, "You may be the only
Bible someone ever reads."

Mary Pielenz Hampton

We continually remember before
our God and Father your work produced
by faith, your labor prompted by love,
and your endurance inspired by hope
in our Lord Jesus Christ.

1 Thessalonians 1:3